AMERICAN FOOTBALL
OFFICIAL ANNUAL

PHOTOGRAPHS: All photographs are copyright © NFL Properties Ltd.
Cover photograph of Joe Montana taken by Peter Brouillet.

Editor: Sheila Cranna

Designer: Gary Gilbert

The Super Bowl – more than just a game!

The Super Bowl is more than a football game to American football fans. It's a national holiday combining aspects of a Carnival, beer festival and World Cup.

Once just an American sporting event, it is now watched on millions of television sets around the world.

Wives who cursed their husbands throughout the professional football season for watching a game every Sunday will willingly sit next to them to view this game on this special Sunday every January. Millions more will crowd into their favourite restaurants and bars to cheer on their favourite team.

How did this unique celebration of American life come about?

It began at an airport in Dallas, Texas, born of a desire for peace between the established National Football League and the upstart American Football League. Since its inception

Paul Jasienski

George Rose

in 1960, the AFL had fought the NFL in a bidding war for the finest college talent in the land.

Delicate negotiations to achieve peace between the two leagues began in secret when Tex Schramm, general manager of NFL's Dallas Cowboys, met Lamar Hunt, owner of the AFL Kansas City Chiefs, at Love Field.

The date: April 6, 1966.

The meeting place: Schramm's car in the airport parking lot.

The objectives: detente and a possible merger.

"I told him that this was not just conversation, that Pete Rozelle (commissioner of the NFL) knew about it and approved. But I explained that only a few of our owners were aware of it and suggested that he keep it as confidential as possible for a while," Schramm says.

The pace of the peace talks was moving

slowly when New York Giants owner Wellington Mara stunned the pro football world by signing Pete Gogolak, a Hungarian-born placekicker who had played out his option with Buffalo of the AFL.

Until that time, despite their battling for college talent with their chequebooks, the two leagues' owners had refrained from signing each other's talent. But now the war heated up. NFL quarterbacks John Brodie (San Francisco 49ers) and Roman Gabriel (Los Angeles Rams), and tight end Mike Ditka (Chicago Bears) signed with the AFL.

Schramm and Hunt knew they had to achieve peace quickly before the war got out of hand. They met on May 31 at Schramm's home in Dallas. Details of the merger were worked out.

The announcement of a merger of the two leagues came on June 8 at a press conference in New York.

One of the highlights of the press conference was the announcement that the champions of the two leagues would meet in a game at the end of the 1966 season.

It would be billed as "The AFL-NFL World Championship Game," a name which lasted for the first two games, before a new one became official.

The new name was suggested by Hunt, shortly after the announcement of the merger. Hunt, who was so instrumental in achieving peace between the two leagues, had a young daughter who enjoyed bouncing a ball that bounced to unusual heights.

"It's my super ball," she told her father.

Weeks later the league's newly emerged owners were discussing what to call the season-ending game. "The Big One," suggested one owner. "World Championship Game," offered another.

Hunt had a better idea.

"Let's call it the Super Bowl," he said.

A tradition was born.

How the drafts and schedules work

One of the major reasons for the great success of the NFL is the competitive balance among the teams. There is an old saying that, "On any given Sunday, any team in the NFL can beat any other team," and it's true.

This balance – upsets happen frequently, and four different teams have won the Super Bowl in the last four years – translates to greater fan interest. The NFL basically insures equal competition in two ways: by basing the college player draft and the league schedule on the previous season's final standings.

The Super Bowl champion is the king of the professional football world, the best of the 28 teams that make up the two conferences (the American Football Conference and the National Football Conference) of the NFL. But there is a penalty for success. The annual college draft is in reverse order of the standings, with the team having the worst record drafting first and the Super Bowl champion waiting until the twenty-eighth turn. The better your record, the lower your draft position.

Few non-competitive events on the American sports scene command the interest of the draft. Held in New York, it is given great coverage in the newspapers and televised with NFL Commissioner Pete Rozelle presiding. In particular, considerable interest is focussed on the first player chosen in the draft and other players picked in the first of the 12 rounds.

Explaining the draft
To be chosen, a player is required to have graduated from college or to have completed his four years of college eligibility, unless he is a fifth-year student (who sat out of competition for a year), who announces his intention to forgo his final year of eligibility.

Players must sign with the team that selects

Dick Raphael

them in the draft, which virtually all do after a period of contract negotiations. If a player decides not to sign, he must sit out the season, and his name goes back into the draft, where he will be selected by another team the next year.

It was the late Commissioner Bert Bell who initiated the draft in 1936, to help the

Explaining the schedule

To understand how the 16-game regular-season schedule is designed, you must first understand the NFL's structure. The league is split into two 14-team conferences, the National Conference and the American Conference, and each conference is further broken down into two five-team divisions

George Rose

weaker teams by allowing them first choice of the top college talent. Prior to that time, players had been able to sign with any club; and open signing tended to make the strong teams stronger.

The college draft also helps weaker clubs improve in another way. Teams are allowed to trade positions in the draft for current players in the league. A weaker team might trade a high position, such as the third choice in the first round, for a veteran player who could help it right away.

and one four-team division, generally along geographical lines.

Each team plays every other team in its division twice, once at home and once at the other team's home field. But then, the rest of each team's schedule is determined by how it finished in its division the previous season.

The remaining games are scheduled with teams from the other conference and other divisions of the same conference, according to a set formula, which forces the best teams to play each other.

RESULTS AT A GLANCE.

SB I. Green Bay 35, Kansas City 10
Most valuable Player – Bart Starr (Green Bay Quarterback)

SB II. Green Bay 33, Oakland 14
MVP – Bart Starr (Green Bay Quarterback)

SB III. New York Jets 16, Baltimore 7
MVP – Joe Namath (New York Quarterback)

SB IV. Kansas City 23, Minnesota 7
MVP – Len Dawson (Kansas City Quarterback)

SB V. Baltimore 16, Dallas 13
MVP – Chuck Howley (Dallas Linebacker)

SB VI. Dallas 24, Miami 3
MVP – Roger Staubach (Dallas Quarterback)

SB VII. Miami 14, Washington 7
MVP – Jake Scott (Miami Safety)

SB VIII. Miami 24, Minnesota 7
MVP – Larry Csonka (Miami Running Back)

SB IX. Pittsburgh 16, Minnesota 6
MVP – Franco Harris (Pittsburgh Running Back)

SB X. Pittsburgh 21, Dallas 17
MVP – Lynn Swann (Pittsburgh Wide Receiver)

SB XI. Oakland 32, Minnesota 14
MVP – Fred Biletnikoff (Oakland Wide Receiver)

SB XII. Dallas 27, Denver 10
MVPs – Harvey Martin (Dallas Defensive End), Randy White (Dallas Defensive Tackle)

SB XIII. Pittsburgh 35, Dallas 31
MVP – Terry Bradshaw (Pittsburgh Quarterback)

SB XIV. Pittsburgh 31, Los Angeles Rams 19
MVP – Terry Bradshaw (Pittsburgh Quarterback)

SB XV. Oakland 27, Philadelphia 10
MVP – Jim Plunkett (Oakland Quarterback)

SB XVI. San Francisco 26, Cincinatti 21
MVP – Joe Montana (San Francisco Quarterback)

SB XVII. Washington 27, Miami 17
MVP – John Riggins (Washington Running Back)

SB XVIII. Los Angeles Raiders 38, Washington 9
MVP – Marcus Allen (Los Angeles Running Back)

SB XIX. San Francisco 38, Miami 16
MVP – Joe Montana (San Francisco Quarterback)

SB XX. Chicago 46, New England 10
MVP – Richard Dent (Chicago Defensive End)

SB XXI. New York Giants 39, Denver 20
MVP – Phil Simms (New York Quarterback)

SB XXII. Washington 42, Denver 10
MVP – Doug Williams (Washington Quarterback)

SB XXIII. San Francisco 20, Cincinatti 16
MVP – Jerry Rice (San Francisco Wide Receiver)

THE TROPHY

The Super Bowl trophy was first presented to the winners of Super Bowl I – the Green Bay Packers – in 1967. In 1970, it was renamed the Vince Lombardi Trophy to honour one of the game's most respected figures, who died that year.

The trophy – a tapering, triangular base supporting a regulation-size football – is made of sterling silver. It stands over 20 inches high and weighs nearly seven pounds.

Unlike many sports, the winners retain the award permanently, as a new trophy is cast every year.

Chris Hopkins

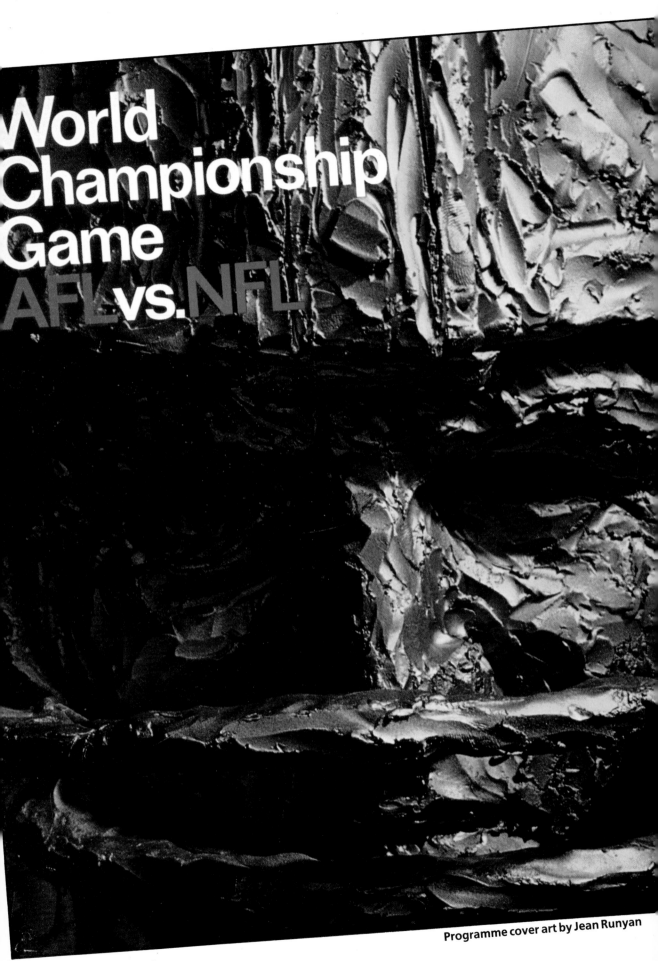

World
Championship
Game
AFL vs. NFL

Programme cover art by Jean Runyan

January 15, 1967
Los Angeles, California

Six months after the merger of the American and National Football Leagues, the champions of the two leagues met for the first time in the Los Angeles Memorial Coliseum, in what was designated officially as the AFL-NFL World Championship Game.

Although the first game failed to sell out, drawing a crowd of 61,946, it would soon have a new name: 'Super Bowl'.

Green Bay, coached by the legendary Vince Lombardi, entered the game as a 13 1/2-point favourite over AFL champion **Kansas City,** coached by Hank Stram. Although the Chiefs held the Packers to a 14-10 margin at halftime, Green Bay's superior manpower eventually led to a 35-10 victory.

Thirty-four-year-old Max McGee of the Packers was the unlikely hero of the first meeting between the two leagues. After catching only four passes for 91 yards and one touchdown during the regular season, McGee expected to spend the entire championship game on the sidelines.

But when Boyd Dowler injured a shoulder on the second play of the game, McGee was sent into action. He caught a 37-yard pass from quarterback Bart Starr for the game's first score, and in the third period, when Green Bay scored twice to put the game out

Elijah Pitts (22), Jerry Kramer (64)

of reach, he added a 13-yard touchdown pass from Starr.

Starr, who passed for 250 yards and two scores, was named the game's most valuable player.

The Chiefs, who outgained the Packers 181 yards to 164 and led in first downs 11-9 in the first half, never threatened after quarterback Len Dawson was intercepted by defensive back Willie Wood early in the third quarter. Wood returned the interception 50 yards to the Chiefs' 5-yard line to set up Elijah Pitts' touchdown that made it 21-10.

Bart Starr, Most Valuable Player

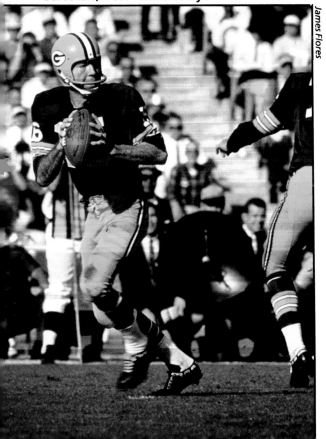

SCORING SUMMARY:

Kansas City	0	10	0	0	10
Green Bay	7	7	14	7	35

GB — McGee 37 pass from Starr (Chandler kick)
KC — McClinton 7 pass from Dawson (Mercer kick)
GB — Taylor 14 run (Chandler kick)
KC — FG Mercer 31
GB — Pitts 5 run (Chandler kick)
GB — McGee 13 pass from Starr (Chandler kick)
GB — Pitts 1 run (Chandler kick)

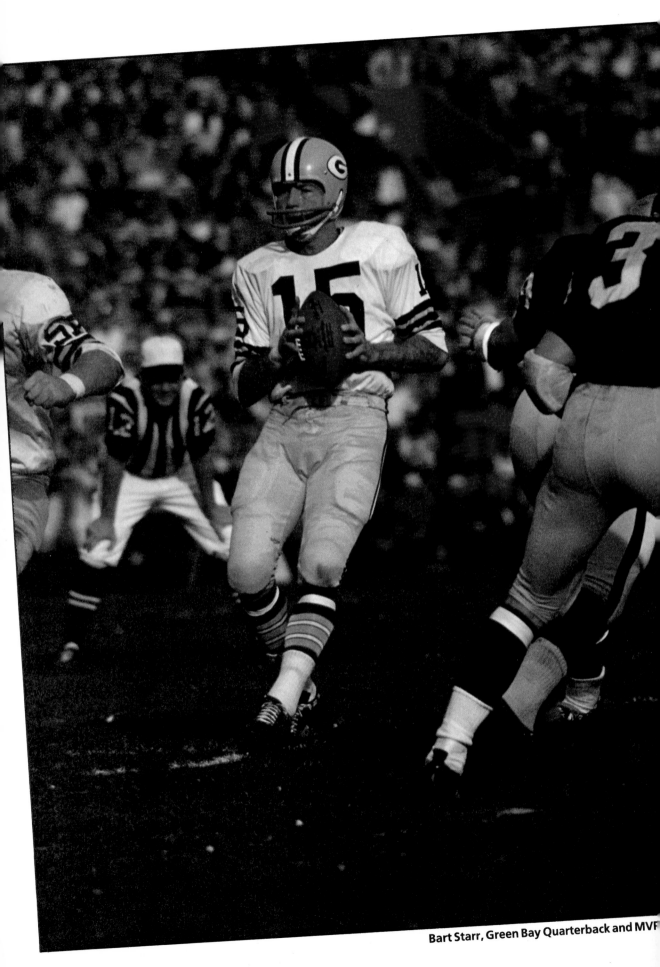

Bart Starr, Green Bay Quarterback and MVF

**January 14, 1968
Miami, Florida**

Once again the champions of the established National Football League, the **Green Bay Packers** had little trouble winning their second consecutive world championship with a 33-14 victory over AFL champion **Oakland.**

Quarterback Bart Starr, again named the most valuable player, repeated his fine effort of the first championship game by completing 13 of 24 passes for 202 yards and one touchdown. Starr also was responsible for the Packers converting 6 of 11 crucial third-down situations.

Placekicker Don Chandler also had a big day, connecting on four field goals, including a 39-yarder to open the scoring on Green Bay's first possession of the game.

In warm weather conditions at the Orange Bowl – 86 degrees – the Packers continued to dominate the action on their second possession of the game. Holding the ball for 8 minutes and 40 seconds, Green Bay marched 84 yards from its own 3 to the Raiders' 13 in 17 plays. When the drive stalled, Chandler kicked a 20-yard field goal.

Green Bay tacked 13 more points on the scoreboard in the second period while holding the Raiders to a touchdown. A spectacular 62-yard pass from Starr to split end Boyd Dowler increased the Packers' lead to 13-0. Oakland trimmed the lead to 13-7 when quarterback Daryle Lamonica hit end Bill Miller with a 23-yard touchdown pass, but Green Bay led by 16-7 at half-time.

The Packers broke open the game in the third quarter just as they had done in Super Bowl I against Kansas City. They went 82 yards in 11 plays on their second possession with Donny Anderson scoring from the 2-yard line to make the score 23-7.

Ron Wolin

Theme art

The game became a rout when Chandler connected on a 31-yard field goal and defensive back Herb Adderley intercepted a Lamonica pass and ran it back 60 yards for Green Bay's final score.

Following his second consecutive world championship, Packers head coach Vince Lombardi announced he was retiring to become the team's full-time general manager.

SCORING SUMMARY:

Green Bay	3	13	10	7	**33**
Oakland	0	7	0	7	**14**

GB – FG Chandler 39
GB – FG Chandler 20
GB – Dowler 62 pass from Starr (Chandler kick)
Oak – Miller 23 pass from Lamonica (Blanda kick)
GB – FG Chandler 43
GB – Anderson 2 run (Chandler kick)
GB – FG Chandler 31
GB – Adderley 60 interception (Chandler kick)
Oak – Miller 23 pass from Lamonica (Blanda kick)

The Orange Bowl, site of Super Bowls II, III V, X, XIII

Al Messerschmidt

Theme art by Peter Palombi

January 12, 1969
Miami, Florida

Three days before Super Bowl III, the first one to carry the title, **New York Jets** quarterback Joe Namath concluded an awards ceremony by saying:

"And we're going to win Sunday, I'll guarantee you."

The remark proved to be prophetic when Namath led his team to a 16-7 upset over **Baltimore** at the Orange Bowl, the AFL's first victory over the NFL in the world championship game. Namath was named the game's most valuable player.

Namath's remarks made national headlines and focused attention on a game that was supposed to be more lopsided than Green Bay's easy victories over Kansas City and Oakland. Namath's arm was as good as his mouth with the quarterback becoming a national sports figure by completing 17 of 28 passes for 206 yards.

Field goals of 32, 30 and 9 yards by Jim Turner and one touchdown enabled the surprising Jets to take a 16-0 lead into the final quarter. Until that point the only touchdown of the game occurred in the second quarter when fullback Matt Snell scored from four yards out, concluding an 80-yard, 12-play drive.

Snell would finish the game with a record 121 yards on 30 plays with the game being played at the Orange Bowl for the second consecutive year.

In the first half, the Colts moved inside the Jets' 20-yard line three times without scoring. Baltimore finally scored its only touchdown with 3:19 left in the game when fullback Jerry Hill went over from the one.

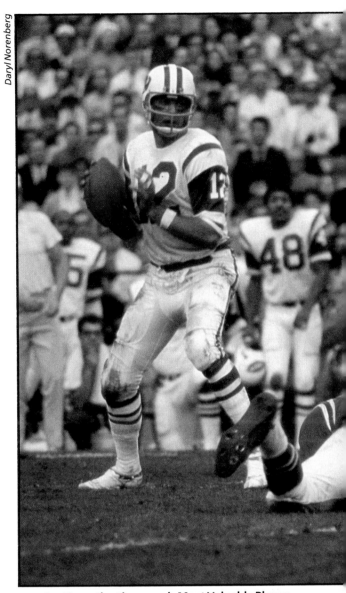

Daryl Norenberg

Joe Namath – the game's Most Valuable Player

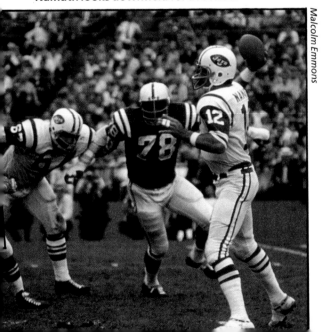

Namath looks downfield for a receiver

Malcolm Emmons

It was a stunning upset. Under head coach Don Shula Baltimore had lost only one of its 14 NFL regular season games. Weeb Ewbank's Jets were 11-3 before defeating Oakland for the AFL title.

After being so vocal before the game, Namath at first refused to talk to some writers in the dressing room following the victory. "If you had seen us all year, you wouldn't have been surprised," he told writers from NFL cities.

SCORING SUMMARY:

NY Jets	0	7	6	3	16
Baltimore	0	0	0	7	7

NYJ – Snell 4 run (J. Turner kick)
NYJ – FG J. Turner 32
NYJ – FG J. Turner 30
NYJ – FG J. Turner 9
Balt – Hill 1 run (Michaels kick)

86 – Buck Buchanan; 41 – Dave Osborn

January 11, 1970
New Orleans, Lousiana

Under extreme pressure, quarterback Len Dawson led **Kansas City** to a 23-7 victory over **Minnesota** for a second consecutive upset by an AFL team.

Dawson had missed six regular-season games with a knee injury. Then, five days before the world championship game at Tulane Stadium, his name had been linked to a federal government gambling investigation.

But he played like a man who didn't have a care in the world.

Although they were two-touchdown underdogs, the Chiefs never trailed in the game to gain a measure of revenge for their loss to Green Bay in Super Bowl I. Dawson completed 12 of 17 passes for 142 yards and a 46-yard touchdown to Otis Taylor in the third quarter after the Vikings had closed to 16-7.

Programme cover art by Don Weller

Len Dawson – the game's Most Valuable Player

Tony Tomsic

Dawson, who was named the Super Bowl's most valuable player, later was cleared in the gambling investigation.

Jan Stenerud of Norway, one of the first soccer-style kickers in professional football, played a key role for the Chiefs. On Kansas City's first possession of the game Stenerud hit a 48-yard field goal to give the Chiefs a 3-0 lead.

When the Chiefs took over the ball the next time, they moved 55 yards before Stenerud hit on a 32-yard field goal to make it 6-0. Stenerud remained hot, hitting a 25-yarder on Kansas City's next possession for a 9-0 lead to stun the Vikings.

The Chiefs continued to pour it on. With time running out late in the first half, halfback Mike Garrett scored from five yards out on a misdirection play to make it 16-0. The Chiefs' line pulled in one direction; the Vikings gave pursuit; and Garrett went against the grain to score.

SCORING SUMMARY:

Minnesota	0	0	7	0	7
Kansas City	3	13	7	0	23

KC – FG Stenerud 48
KC – FG Stenerud 32
KC – FG Stenerud 25
KC – Garrett 5 run (Stenerud kick)
Minn – Osborn 4 run (Cox kick)
KC – Taylor 46 pass from Dawson (Stenerud kick)

SUPER BOWL V

ce $1.50

WORLD PROFESSIONAL FOOTBALL CHAMPIONSHIP
FOR THE VINCE LOMBARDI TROPHY
Sunday, January 17, 1971 • 2:00 p.m. Orange Bowl, Miami

Programme cover artist Howard Rogers

January 17, 1971
Miami, Florida

Jim O'Brien won the war of nerves and Baltimore won the game 16-13 over the **Dallas Cowboys.**

With nine seconds left in the game and the score tied 13-13, O'Brien entered the game to attempt a game-winning 32-yard field goal. The Cowboys called time out.

When play resumed, Dallas attempted to call time out again to unnerve O'Brien. Referee Norm Schachter informed the Cowboys they could not call successive time outs without a play being run.

When Earl Morrall, who had replaced starting Colts quarterback Johnny Unitas midway through the game, kneeled to take the snap, O'Brien whispered, "The wind . . . the wind?"

"There is no wind," Morrall replied. "Just kick the ball straight."

O'Brien's kick went through the uprights just five seconds ahead of the final gun at the Orange Bowl.

Some thought the Colts were lucky to win the game. "So what?" said tackle Bob Vogel. "I've had luck decide against us so many times I'm sick of it. I quit being proud years ago when we lost games we should have won.

"The way I look at it, we're going to get the Super Bowl ring because we won the games that counted this year. We deserve it."

Dallas opened the game's scoring when Mike Clark kicked a 14-yard field goal for a 3-0 lead with 5:32 left in the first quarter. Eight seconds into the second quarter the Cowboys scored again on a 30-yard field goal by Clark to make it 6-0.

The Colts got back into the game 42 seconds later on a freak play. Unitas threw a medium-deep pass to wide receiver Eddie Hinton, who tipped the ball. Cowboys defensive back Mel Renfro also tipped the ball.

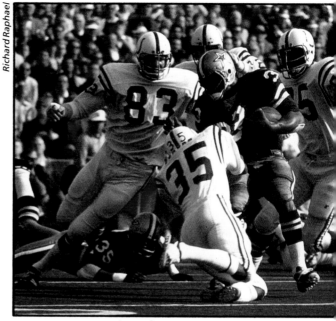

Richard Raphael

Colts Defence stop Duane Thomas

Colts tight end John Mackey, who was running free behind the defence, caught the ball at Dallas' 45-yard line. Running untouched, Mackey went all the way for a touchdown. The conversion was blocked, leaving the score tied 6-6.

The Cowboys regained the lead (13-6) at half-time, and Baltimore scored a touchdown in the fourth quarter to tie it again at 13-13.

For the only time in a Super Bowl, a player from the losing team – linebacker Chuck Howley – was named the game's MVP.

SCORING SUMMARY:

Baltimore	0	6	0	10	16
Dallas	3	10	0	0	13

Dall – FG Clark 14
Dall – FG Clark 30
Balt – Mackey 75 pass from Unitas (kick blocked)
Dall – Thomas 7 pass from Morton (Clark kick)
Balt – Nowatzke 2 run (O'Brien kick)
Balt – FG O'Brien 32

John Unitas

Tony Tomsic

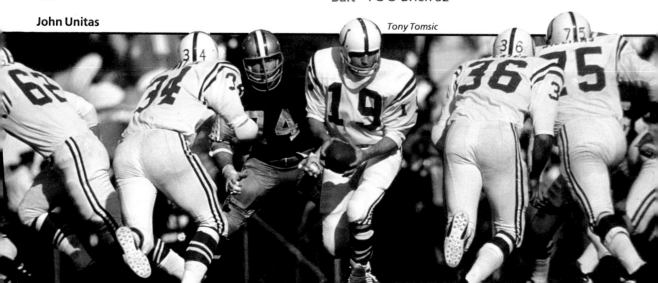

Malcolm Emmons

MVP Roger Staubach scrambles for yar

January 16, 1972
New Orleans, Louisiana

Tom Landry picked up his first Super Bowl victory as a head coach when his **Dallas Cowboys** set a Super Bowl rushing record of 252 yards on their way to a 24-3 victory over **Miami** at Tulane Stadium.

"My biggest disappointment is that we never challenged," said Miami head coach Don Shula, a Super Bowl loser for the second time. "They completely dominated us."

Duane Thomas, an enigmatic running back who seldom talked to his teammates or the media, was the top runner for the Cowboys, rolling up 95 yards and a touchdown on 19 plays. Walt Garrison added 74 yards on the ground, while quarterback Roger Staubach, the game's most valuable player, passed for 119 yards and two touchdowns.

Dallas took a 3-0 lead with 1:23 left in the first quarter when Mike Clark kicked a nine-yard field goal. The Cowboys built on their lead with a 76-yard, 10-play drive that culminated with a seven-yard touchdown pass from Staubach to wide receiver Lance Alworth in the corner of the end zone with 1:15 remaining in the half.

Duane Thomas (33)

Malcolm Emmons

Programme cover design by Mike Gaines

But Miami got on the scoreboard with only four seconds left in the first half when Garo Yepremian booted a 31-yard field goal after the Dolphins drove 44 yards in five plays.

The Cowboys went right to work after taking the second half kickoff. A three-yard run by Thomas capped a 71-yard drive in eight plays, raising the Dallas advantage to 17-3.

Early in the fourth quarter Staubach passed seven yards to Mike Ditka for the final score of the game.

SCORING SUMMARY:

Dallas	3	7	7	7	24
Miami	0	3	0	0	3

Dall – FG Clark 9
Dall – Alworth 7 pass from Staubach (Clark kick)
Mia – FG Yepremian 31
Dall – D. Thomas 3 run (Clark kick)
Dall – Ditka 7 pass from Staubach (Clark kick)

SUPER BOWL VII

AFC VS. NFC FOR THE NFL CHAMPIONSHIP AND THE VINCE LOMBARDI TROPHY
SUNDAY, JANUARY 14, 1973 12:30 P.M. · LOS ANGELES MEMORIAL COLISEUM

$2.00

Programme cover art by Howard Rogers

January 14, 1973
Los Angeles, California

It was the Year of the Dolphins.

Capping a perfect season in which they went 17-0, **Miami** defeated **Washington** 14-7 before 90,182 fans at Memorial Coliseum to become the first perfect-record team in NFL history.

The victory, not as close as the score indicates, erased the stigma of two previous Super Bowl losses for Dolphins head coach Don Shula. "The pressure's off," Shula said afterward. "I was aware of the reputation I had gotten ... the losses were there; you couldn't hide from them.

"But that's all in the past."

Playing conservative football – quarterback Bob Griese passed only 11 times for 88 yards and a touchdown – the Dolphins took a 7-0 lead the third time they had the ball. On the next to last play of the first quarter, Griese found wide receiver Howard Twilley with a 28-yard scoring pass.

Miami appeared to score in the second quarter on a 47-yard pass from Griese to wide receiver Paul Warfield, but another wide receiver was detected moving forward before the snap of the ball and the play was nullified.

Middle linebacker Nick Buoniconti of the Dolphins set up the next score when he intercepted a pass by Redskins quarterback Billy Kilmer and returned the ball 32 yards to Washington's 27.

The Dolphins scored with 18 seconds left in the half on the fifth play after Buoniconti's interception. Jim Kiick went across from the one-yard line to give Miami a 14-0 advantage.

Washington's only touchdown came in the fourth quarter on a freak play. Miami had the ball on the Washington 34 with Garo Yepremian attempting a 42-yard field goal.

Garo Yepremian

The snap from centre Howard Kindig was low and holder Earl Morrall had to place the ball quickly.

Yepremian's kick was low and defensive tackle Bill Brundige blocked the attempt. Yepremian picked up the ball and attempted to pass, but the ball slipped out of his hand and into the air. Washington's Mike Bass caught it and ran 49 yards for a touchdown with 2:07 left.

Miami safety Jake Scott, who had two interceptions, was named the most valuable player.

SCORING SUMMARY:

Miami	7	7	0	0	14
Washington	0	0	0	7	7

Mia – Twilley 28 pass from Griese (Yepremian kick)
Mia – Kiick 1 run (Yepremian kick)
Wash – Bass 49 fumble return (Knight kick)

Jake Scott, Miami Safety and MVP

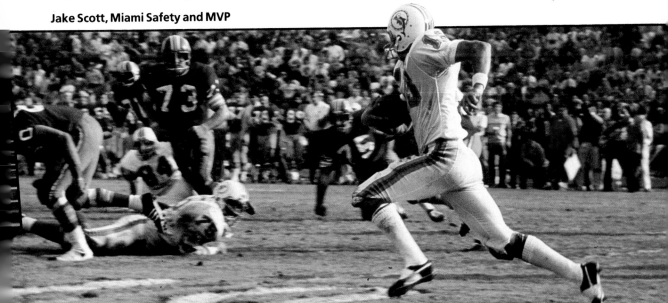

Malcolm Emmons

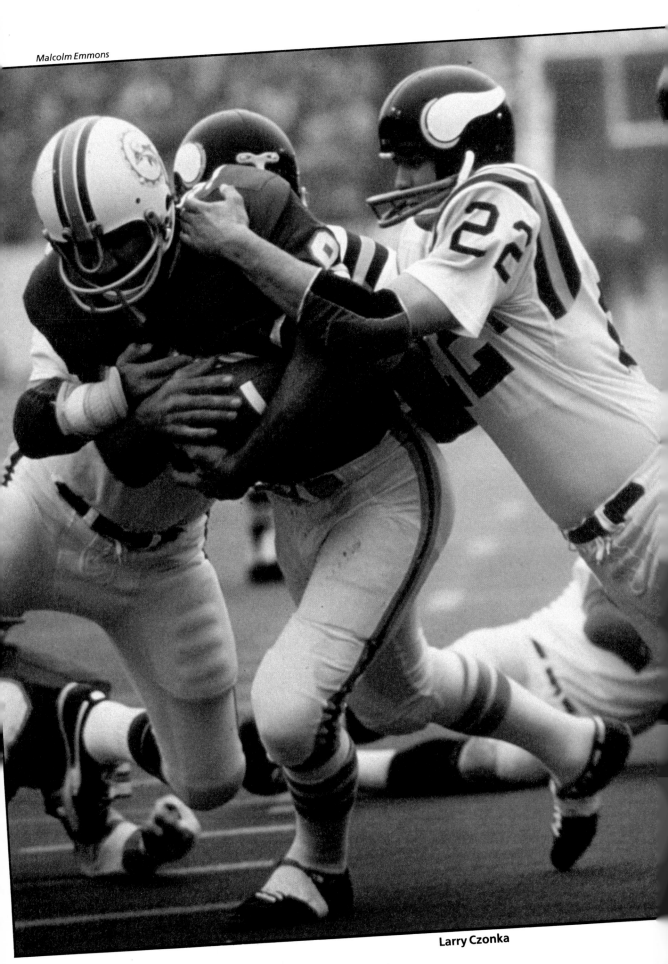

Larry Czonka

**January 13, 1974
Houston, Texas**

Behind the running of Larry Csonka, **Miami** equalled Green Bay's victories in Super Bowls I and II by rolling over the **Minnesota Vikings** 24-7 at Rice Stadium.

Csonka carried the football 33 times for 145 yards and two touchdowns and was picked as the game's MVP. Quarterback Bob Griese was called on to pass only seven times, completing six for just 73 yards.

But Griese was the Super Bowl-winning quarterback for the second year in succession and there was talk that the Dolphins were stronger than Vince Lombardi's great Packers teams.

"I don't know about legends and statistics," said Csonka. "Football is a 'now' game; that's all that matters."

While Griese was passing only seven times, his Vikings counterpart, Fran Tarkenton, was busy filling the air with footballs as the Vikings' ground game was held to 72 yards. Tarkenton hit on 18 of 28 passes for 182 yards and had one pass intercepted.

Miami was in control from the opening kick-off. Csonka capped a 10-play drive with a five-yard run for the game's first score. After Minnesota ran three plays and was forced to punt, the Dolphins scored again at the end of a 10-play drive. Jim Kiick scored on a one-yard run to make it 14-0.

Czonka – Most Valuable Player

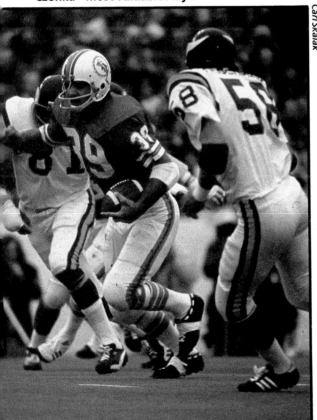

Carl Skalak

Programme cover art by Peter Palombi

A 28-yard field goal by Garo Yepremian late in the first half raised Miami's lead to 17-0 at the break.

Csonka got his second touchdown in the third quarter on a two-yard run up the middle.

Minnesota scored its only touchdown after a drive that began on the Vikings' 43-yard line with 1:34 left in the third quarter and concluded with Tarkenton's four-yard run 1:35 into the final quarter.

SCORING SUMMARY:

Minnesota	0	0	0	7	7
Miami	14	3	7	0	24

Mia – Csonka 5 run (Yepremian kick)
Mia – Kiick 1 run (Yepremian kick)
Mia – FG Yepremian 28
Mia – Csonka 2 run (Yepremian kick)
Minn – Tarkenton 4 run (Cox kick)

Tony Tomsic

Dwight White (78) and Jack Lambert (58) stop Dave Osborn (41)

January 12, 1975
New Orleans, Louisiana

Tulane Stadium was the scene for a great performance by fullback Franco Harris of the **Pittsburgh Steelers,** who won a championship for the first time in the club's 42-year history.

Harris rushed 34 times for 158 yards, both Super Bowl records, and was chosen the game's most valuable player. The **Vikings** lost for the third time without a victory.

Neither team was able to score a touchdown in the first half of play, but Pittsburgh was able to take a 2-0 lead into the break. With 7:11 left in the second quarter, Minnesota quarterback Fran Tarkenton fumbled a hand-off to running back Dave Osborn.

Attempting to regain possession of the ball, Tarkenton slid into the end zone, where he was downed by defensive end Dwight White for a safety.

Another fumble allowed Pittsburgh to score at the beginning of the second half. Bill Brown of the Vikings mishandled the second-half kick-off, and Pittsburgh's Marv Kellum recovered at the Minnesota 30. Harris scored on a nine-yard run to increase his team's lead to 9-0.

There was no further scoring until the final quarter. Minnesota linebacker Matt Blair blocked Bobby Walden's punt at the 15-yard

Franco Harris carries the ball

Theme art by Bart Forbes

line, and the ball was recovered in the end zone by the Vikings' Terry Brown for a touchdown with 10:33 left in the game.

Fred Cox's extra point attempt hit the left upright and the score remained 9-6.

Beginning on their own 34-yard line and, with quarterback Terry Bradshaw completing a critical 30-yard pass to tight end Larry Brown, the Steelers moved to their final touchdown of the game. Bradshaw passed four yards to Brown for the score.

SCORING SUMMARY:

Pittsburgh	0	2	7	7 16
Minnesota	0	0	0	6 6

Pitt — Safety, White downed Tarkenton in end zone
Pitt — Harris 9 run (Gerela kick)
Minn — T. Brown recovered blocked punt in end zone (kick failed)
Pitt — L. Brown 4 pass from Bradshaw (Gerela kick)

Photo by Stan Kaplan

January 18, 1976
Miami, Florida

In a game rated the most exciting Super Bowl so far, **Pittsburgh** won its second consecutive world title 21-17 over **Dallas** on quarterback Terry Bradshaw's 64-yard touchdown pass to wide receiver Lynn Swann with 3:02 remaining at the Orange Bowl.

The touchdown gave the Steelers a 21-10 lead, but the issue remained in doubt until the final gun. Dallas took over on its 20-yard line with 2:54 left in the game and scored in only five plays on quarterback Roger Staubach's 34-yard pass to wide receiver Percy Howard.

And the Cowboys still weren't finished.

After stopping Pittsburgh on its final possession, the Cowboys had a chance to win the game until a Staubach pass was intercepted in the end zone by safety Glen Edwards.

Dallas led most of the game and might have won except for arousing the ire of the Steelers' great linebacker, Jack Lambert. In the third quarter, Pittsburgh's Roy Gerela missed his second field-goal attempt of the game. Safety Cliff Harris of the Cowboys mockingly patted the kicker on the helmet. Incensed, Lambert threw Harris to the ground and played the rest of the game like a madman.

Pittsburgh wide receiver Lynn Swann

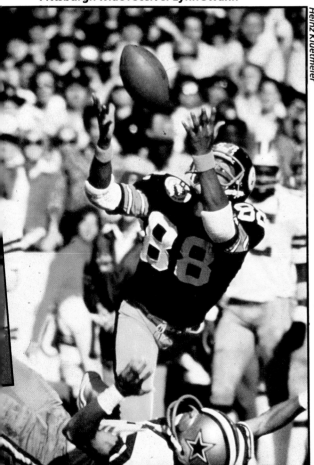

Heinz Kluetmeier

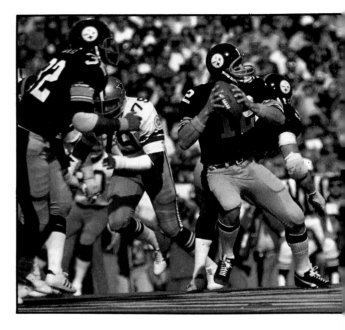

"I felt like we were intimidated a little in the first half," the linebacker explained after the game. "The Pittsburgh Steelers aren't supposed to be intimidated. We are supposed to do the intimidating. I decided to do something about it."

Dallas scored first after a fumbled punt attempt by the Steelers. On the next play, Staubach threw a 29-yard touchdown pass to wide receiver Drew Pearson with only 4:36 gone in the game.

The Steelers struck back quickly, moving 67 yards on eight plays on the next series. Tight end Randy Grossman caught a seven-yard touchdown pass from Bradshaw.

It was the Cowboys' turn on the next series. Toni Fritsch kicked a 36-yard field goal to put Dallas ahead, 10-7, and that's how it remained until the exciting final period that saw 21 points scored.

Swann, who had four catches for 161 yards, was voted the game's most valuable player.

SCORING SUMMARY:

Dallas	7	3	0	7	17
Pittsburgh	7	0	0	14	21

Dall — D. Pearson 29 pass from Staubach (Fritsch kick)
Pitt — Grossman 7 pass from Bradshaw (Gerela kick)
Dall — FG Fritsch 36
Pitt — Safety, Harrison blocked Hoopes's punt through the end zone
Pitt — FG Gerela 36
Pitt — FG Gerela 18
Pitt — Swann 64 pass from Bradshaw (kick failed)
Dall — P. Howard 34 pass from Staubach (Fritsch kick)

Tony Tomsic

Fred Biletnikoff, Oakland Wide Receiver and the game's MVP

January 9, 1977
Pasadena, California

For Fran Tarkenton and the **Minnesota Vikings** it was the same old story: a different opponent but the same result. This time the opponent was the **Oakland Raiders** and the loss was by 32-14 before 100,421 at the Rose Bowl.

It was the Vikings' and head coach Bud Grant's fourth defeat without a victory in the Super Bowl.

Oakland used a strong rushing attack, led by running back Clarence Davis, to roll up 429 yards, 266 on the ground. Davis gained 137 yards on 16 carries for a career high and fullback Mark van Eeghen added 73 on 18 carries. Most of the yardage came behind blocking on the left side from tackle Art Shell and guard Gene Upshaw.

"When you've got the horses you ride them," quarterback Ken Stabler said, referring to Shell and Upshaw. "We're not a fancy team. We just line up and try to knock you out of there. No one is better at it than those two guys."

The Raiders established their dominance on the opening series of the game. They moved from their own 34 to the Minnesota 11 in eight plays. On fourth down, Errol Mann attempted a 29-yard field goal, but the ball hit the left upright and the attempt failed.

"Don't worry," Stabler told head coach John Madden, "there's more where that came from."

Stabler was right.

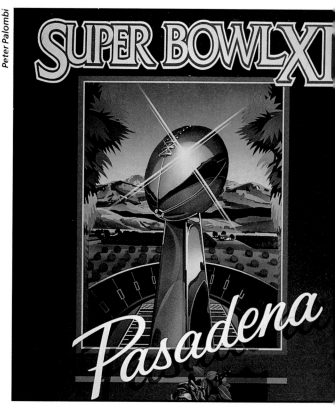

Peter Palombi

Theme art

Using the last 4:35 of the first quarter and the first 48 seconds of the second period, the Raiders drove 90 yards in 12 plays to set up a 24-yard field goal by Mann and led 3-0.

On its next possession, Oakland advanced 64 yards in 10 plays, tight end Dave Casper scoring on a one-yard pass from Stabler for the game's first touchdown and a 10-0 lead.

A short touchdown run, one yard, by running back Pete Banaszak gave the Raiders a 16-0 lead at the intermission.

The onslaught continued in the second half. Mann hit another field goal, this one from 40 yards out, late in the third quarter to make it 19-0 and the Raiders added 13 points in the final period.

Oakland wide receiver Fred Biletnikoff, who contributed four critical catches, was chosen the game's MVP.

SCORING SUMMARY:

Oakland	0	16	3	13	32
Minnesota	0	0	7	7	14

Oak – FG Mann 24
Oak – Casper 1 pass from Stabler (Mann kick)
Oak – Banaszak 1 run (kick failed)
Oak – FG Mann 40
Minn – S. White 8 pass from Tarkenton (Cox kick)
Oak – Banaszak 2 run (Mann kick)
Oak – Brown 75 interception return (kick failed)
Minn – Voight 13 pass from Lee (Cox kick)

Clarence Davis (28), Oakland Running Back

Tony Tomsic

Roger Staubach

January 15, 1978
New Orleans, Louisiana

Dallas beat **Denver** at its own game and emerged with a 27-10 victory over the Broncos to even its Super Bowl record at 2-2 before 75,583 in the Superdome.

The Cowboys' defence paralysed the Broncos' attack in the first half, intercepting four of Craig Morton's passes and recovering three fumbles. Morton was limited to 39 yards passing in the game, and his replacement at quarterback, Norris Weese, was able to add only 22. Cowboys defensive tackle Randy White and defensive end Harvey Martin shared the most valuable player award.

"They played the kind of game we usually play," said Morton. "They beat us at our own game – taking turnovers. So many times this season other teams gave us all those turnovers. Today it was just our turn [to give the ball away]."

The second quarter illustrates the kind of day it was for Denver. The last five times the Broncos had the ball they turned it over to the Cowboys, who amassed 325 yards in total offence for the game to Denver's 156.

Naturally, the mistakes caught up with the Broncos. Dallas safety Randy Hughes intercepted a Morton pass midway through the first quarter to put the Cowboys on the Denver 25. Five plays later Tony Dorsett scored the game's first touchdown from three yards out.

On the next series, Morton was intercepted again, this time by cornerback Aaron Kyle. The Denver defence stiffened and Dallas was forced to settle for a 35-yard field goal by Efren Herrera and a 10-0 lead. Minutes later,

Touchdown catch by Butch Johnson

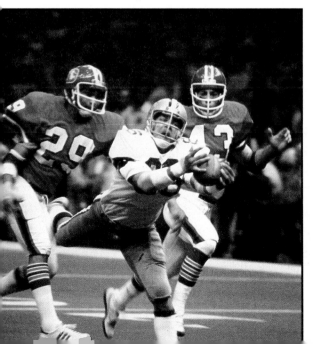

Theme art by Donald Moss

Herrera connected on another field goal, from 43 yards out, for a 13-0 halftime advantage.

Denver finally got on the scoreboard in the third quarter. Jim Turner hit a 47-yard field goal, but Dallas countered by marching 58 yards for a score, most of it coming on a 45-yard touchdown pass to Butch Johnson, who made a spectacular diving catch in the end zone. That made it 20-3, and Denver could never catch up.

SCORING SUMMARY:

Dallas	10	3	7	7	27
Denver	0	0	10	0	10

Dall – Dorsett 3 run (Herrera kick)
Dall – FG Herrera 35
Dall – FG Herrera 43
Den – FG Turner 47
Dall – Johnson 45 pass from Staubach (Herrera kick)
Den – Lytle 1 run (Turner kick)
Dall – Richards 29 pass from Newhouse (Herrera kick)

John Biever

Franco Harris (32) rushed for 68 yards; Ed Jones (72)

**January 21, 1979
Miami, Florida**

This game provided a number of "firsts". It was the first time two teams had met in a rematch. And, with a 35-31 victory over **Dallas, Pittsburgh** became the first team to win three Super Bowls. It also was the highest-scoring Super Bowl.

As 79,484 fans watched, quarterback Terry Bradshaw was the big man for the Steelers, tossing four touchdown passes and gaining a personal-high 318 yards through the air. He broke Bart Starr's Super Bowl passing yardage record by halftime, throwing for 253 yards and three touchdowns. Naturally, he was voted the game's most valuable player.

The Dallas offence, with quarterback Roger Staubach throwing for 228 yards and three touchdowns, was pretty potent itself. The Cowboys netted 330 yards, only 27 less than the Steelers.

The tone was set on the first series of the game when Bradshaw fired a 28-yard touchdown pass to John Stallworth. The 7-0 lead lasted until Staubach found wide receiver Tony Hill with a 39-yard touchdown pass on the final play of the first quarter.

Dallas took its only lead of the game at 14-7 when linebacker Mike Hegmen wrestled the ball away from Bradshaw early in the second quarter and ran 37 yards for a touchdown.

Three plays later the explosive game was tied again. Bradshaw hit Stallworth with another touchdown pass, good for 75 yards, and it was 14-14.

Pittsburgh regained the lead with only 26 seconds left in the half, after cornerback Mel Blount intercepted a Staubach pass and returned it to the 29. After a penalty and two long gainers to Lynn Swan, Bradshaw hit running back Rocky Bleir with a seven-yard scoring pass.

Preliminary art by Peter Lloyd

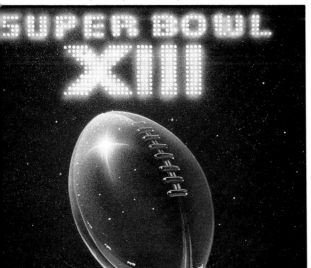

Vernon J. Biever

Pittsburgh's Franco Harris

A 27-yard field goal by the Cowboys' Rafael Septien was the only score in the third quarter.

The two teams exploded for 28 points in the final 15 minutes. Pittsburgh got its two touchdowns in a 19-second span. It started when Franco Harris scored on a 22-yard run. Dallas fumbled the ensuing kickoff and Pittsburgh recovered. Bradshaw immediately tossed an 18-yard touchdown pass to Swann for what turned out to be the winning points when the Cowboys also scored 14 points in the last quarter.

SCORING SUMMARY:

Pittsburgh	7	14	0	14	35
Dallas	7	7	3	14	31

Pitt — Stallworth 28 pass from Bradshaw (Gerela kick)
Dall — Hill 39 pass from Staubach (Septien kick)
Dall — Hegman 37 fumble return (Septien kick)
Pitt — Stallworth 75 pass from Bradshaw (Gerela kick)
Pitt — Bleier 7 pass from Bradshaw (Gerela kick)
Dall — FG Septien 27
Pitt — Harris 22 run (Gerela kick)
Pitt — Swann 18 pass from Bradshaw (Gerela kick)
Dall — DuPree 7 pass from Staubach (Septien kick)
Dall — B. Johnson 4 pass from Staubach (Septien kick)

Amos Love

John Stallworth catches the game-clinching touchdown

January 20, 1980
Pasadena, California

A familiar script was unveiled before 103,985 fans at Pasadena's historic Rose Bowl. The cast of characters remained the same: quarterback Terry Bradshaw, wide receiver John Stallworth, and the **Pittsburgh Steelers.**

Even the ending remained the same: a Steelers victory, their fourth since first appearing in the Super Bowl in January of 1975.

The director's role was also unchanged with head coach Chuck Noll producing the dramatic 31-19 Steelers victory over the **Los Angeles Rams** with Bradshaw in the starring role.

Los Angeles, led by a movie-handsome quarterback named Vince Ferragama, actually went into the final 15 minutes of the game with a 19-17 lead.

Intercepted three times in the game, Bradshaw rebounded by throwing a 73-yard touchdown pass to Stallworth with 2:56 gone in the final period for the game-winner. Then, after the Bradshaw-Stallworth connection worked again for 45 yards, Franco Harris scored an insurance touchdown on a one-yard run.

Bradshaw wound up with 14 completions in 21 attempts for 309 yards and was voted the most valuable player for the second time.

But it wasn't easy for the Steelers, who scored first in the opening quarter on a 41-yard field goal by Matt Bahr. Los Angeles came back quickly on the following series with running back Cullen Bryant going over from the one.

Chuck Ren

HOLLYWOOD

Theme art

Terry Bradshaw (12) hands off to Rocky Bleier

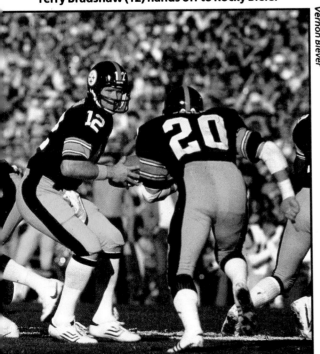

Vernon Biever

In the second quarter the Rams scored six points on 31 and 45-yard field goals by Frank Corral, but the Steelers picked up seven on a one-yard touchdown run by Harris and a successful Bahr conversion.

Both teams scored a single touchdown in the third quarter, setting the stage for Bradshaw's fourth-quarter heroics.

SCORING SUMMARY:

L.A. Rams	7	6	6	0	19
Pittsburgh	3	7	7	14	31

Pitt – FG Bahr 41
Rams – Bryant 1 run (Corral kick)
Pitt – Harris 1 run (Bahr kick)
Rams – FG Corral 31
Rams – FG Corral 45
Pitt – Swann 47 pass from Bradshaw (Bahr kick)
Rams – R. Smith 24 pass from McCutcheon (kick failed)
Pitt – Stallworth 73 pass from Bradshaw (Bahr kick)
Pit – Harris 1 run (Bahr kick)

Michael Zagaris

Touchdown catch by Cliff Branch

January 25, 1981
New Orleans, Louisiana

Stan Kaplan

Oakland became the first wild-card team to win the Super Bowl, when linebacker Rod Martin intercepted three **Philadelphia** passes to key a 27-10 victory over Philadelphia at the Superdome. In the NFL play-off system, a wild-card team is one that failed to win a division championship, but qualified on the basis of its won-loss record.

Martin's interceptions led to 10 points and controlled the tempo of the game. Veteran quarterback Jim Plunkett also played a big role for the Raiders, throwing three touchdown passes while completing 13 of 21 attempts for 261 yards and no interceptions. Plunkett was voted the game's MVP.

Martin, however, made his presence felt immediately. On the third play of the game, Martin intercepted quarterback Ron Jaworski's pass on the Eagles' 47-yard line and returned it to the 30. Seven plays later Plunkett had the Raiders in the end zone on a two-yard pass to wide receiver Cliff Branch.

Noted for their wide-open style of play, the Raiders were pinned deep in their own territory later in the quarter, when Plunkett combined with running back Kenny King for the longest play in Super Bowl history at the time. With the line of scrimmage the Oakland 20, Plunkett hit King with a pass at the 39, and he raced down the left sideline another 61 yards, completing the 80-yard touchdown play.

Theme art

The Eagles held Oakland scoreless in the second quarter while scoring three points on a 30-yard field goal by Tony Franklin.

It was the Raiders' turn again in the third period as they shut out the Eagles while scoring a touchdown and a field goal to take a 24-3 lead. Plunkett and Branch connected for another touchdown, a 29-yarder, and Chris Bahr added a 46-yard field goal.

With the game out of reach, Philadelphia scored its only touchdown in the fourth quarter on an eight-yard pass from Jaworski to tight end Keith Krepfle, while the Raiders had another field goal, from 35 yards out, from Bahr.

SCORING SUMMARY:

Oakland	14	0	10	3	27
Philadelphia	0	3	0	7	10

Oak – Branch 2 pass from Plunkett (Bahr kick)
Oak – King 80 pass from Plunkett (Bahr kick)
Phil – FG Franklin 30
Oak – Branch 29 pass from Plunkett (Bahr kick)
Oak – FG Bahr 46
Phil – Krepfle 8 pass from Jaworski (Franklin kick)
Oak – FG Bahr 35

Jim Plunkett (16) MVP

Manny Rubio

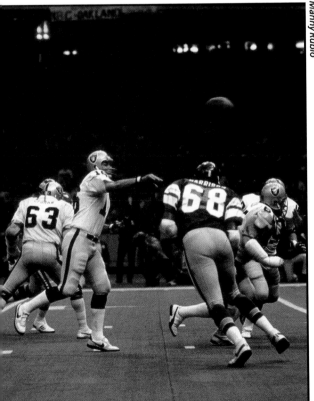

January 24, 1982
Pontiac, Michigan

Ken Anderson sacked by Willie Harper

Noted for its excellent offence, the **San Francisco 49ers** got a surprisingly strong effort from their defence to defeat the explosive **Cincinnati Bengals** 26-21 at the Silverdome in Pontiac, a suburb of Detroit.

San Francisco's defence came up with big plays throughout the game, including a four-play goal line stand late in the third quarter. Meanwhile, Super Bowl most valuable player Joe Montana, the 49ers' quarterback, hit 14 of 22 passes for 157 yards and a touchdown.

Despite the 49ers' victory, the Bengals dominated the statistics with a 356-275 advantage. Montana's quarterback rival, Ken Anderson, completed a record 25 (of 34) passes for 300 yards and two touchdowns. Both touchdown passes were caught by tight end Dan Ross, who had a Super-Bowl-record 11 receptions.

San Francisco safety Dwight Hicks' interception set up the lone touchdown of the opening quarter. A one-yard run by Montana culminated a 68-yard, 11-play drive.

The defence handed the ball to the offence again in the second quarter, when cornerback Eric Wright stripped the ball from Bengals receiver Cris Collingsworth at the 49ers' 8. Twelve plays and 92 yards later, Montana threw an 11-yard touchdown pass to running back Earl Cooper to complete the longest drive so far in Super Bowl history.

4th Down goal line stand

With time running out in the half, Ray Wersching hit field goals of 22 and 26 yards to send San Francisco into the locker room with a 20-0 lead.

Cincinnati finally got on the scoreboard in the third quarter when Anderson scored on a five-yard run, after an 83-yard drive.

Late in the third quarter the Bengals had a first down on the San Francisco 3-yard line. Their inability to score at this point cost them the game when they outscored the 49ers 14-6 in the final quarter.

SCORING SUMMARY:

San Francisco	7	13	0	6	26
Cincinnati	0	0	7	14	21

SF — Montana 1 run (Wersching kick)
SF — Cooper 11 pass from Montana (Wersching kick)
SF — FG Wersching 22
SF — FG Wersching 26
Cin — Anderson 5 run (Breech kick)
Cin — Ross 4 pass from Anderson (Breech kick)
SF — FG Wersching 40
SF — FG Wersching 23
Cin — Ross 3 pass from Anderson (Breech kick)

Messerschmidt

Fulton Walker's kick-off return for a touchdown

January 30, 1983
Pasadena, California

It is traditional for the President of the United States to telephone the locker room of the winning team in the Super Bowl with his congratulations. After **Washington's** 27-17 victory over **Miami** at the Rose Bowl, the most valuable player of the game, John Riggins, said:

"At least for tonight, Ron [Ronald Reagan] may be President, but I'm the King."

Riggins, the lone running back in Washington's offence, performed royally. He gained 166 yards, including a game-winning 43-yard touchdown run in the final quarter.

The Dolphins stunned Washington on their second possession of the game when quarterback David Woodley connected with wide receiver Jimmy Cefalo on a 76-yard touchdown play to take a 7-0 lead.

Both teams scored 10 points in the second quarter. Mark Moseley kicked a 31-yard field goal for the Redskins and Uwe von Schamann countered with a 20-yarder for Miami.

Washington got a touchdown when quarterback Joe Theismann hit wide receiver Alvin Garrett with a four-yard touchdown pass to tie the game at 10-10.

Fulton Walker immediately regained the lead for Miami with the longest kick-off return in Super Bowl history and the first for a touchdown. After Theismann's touchdown pass, Walker took the kick-off and started upfield, angling to his right. Then he suddenly cut back to his left and raced 98 yards for the score which gave the Dolphins a 17-10 half-time lead.

However, the Dolphins wouldn't score another point in the game.

A 20-yard field goal by Moseley cut Miami's lead to 17-13 in the third quarter.

Riggins got his tackle-breaking, winning 43-yard touchdown run in the fourth quarter, and the Redskins added another touchdown on a six-yard pass from Theismann to wide receiver Charlie Brown.

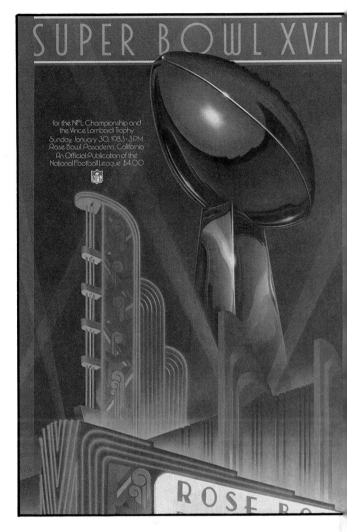

John Riggins to break off his game icing to run

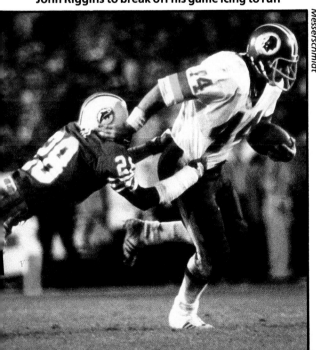

Messerschmidt

SCORING SUMMARY:

Miami	7	10	0	0	17
Washington	0	10	3	14	27

Mia – Cefalo 76 pass from Woodley (von Schamann kick)
Wash – FG Moseley 31
Mia – FG von Schamann 20
Wash – Garrett 4 pass from Theismann (Moseley kick)
Mia – Walker 98 kickoff return (von Schamann kick)
Wash – FG Moseley 20
Wash – Riggins 43 run (Moseley kick)
Wash – Brown 6 pass from Theismann (Moseley kick)

Michael Zaguris

Marcus Allen, Los Angeles Running Back and MVP

January 22, 1984
Tampa, Florida

All three of head coach Tom Flores' platoons – offence, defence, and special teams – contributed to the scoring as the **Los Angeles Raiders** swamped **Washington** 38-9 behind the running of Marcus Allen at Tampa Stadium.

Allen gained a Super-Bowl-record 191 yards on 20 carries and scored twice as the Raiders' defence held Redskins running back John Riggins to 64 yards and a single touchdown.

Early in the first quarter, the Raiders' Derrick Jensen broke through the Redskins' line, blocked Jeff Hayes' punt, and recovered in the end zone to give Los Angeles a 7-0 lead.

Los Angeles increased its advantage to 14-0 in the second quarter when quarterback Jim Plunkett and wide receiver Cliff Branch connected on a 50-yard pass and then on one for 12 yards and a touchdown.

Washington scored on a 24-yard field goal by Mark Moseley, but the Raiders got the points back and more when linebacker Jack Squirek intercepted a Theismann pass and dashed into the end zone from the 5 to make it 21-3 at half-time.

The Redskins got their only touchdown of the game in the third quarter on a one-yard plunge by Riggins, who was held to a 2.5 average on 26 rushing attempts.

John Riggins (44), Howie Long (75)

Riggins' touchdown was more than matched by Allen. The Raiders' running star capped a 70-yard third-quarter drive with a five-yard touchdown run.

Then, on the last play of the quarter, Allen cut loose with the longest run from scrimmage in Super Bowl history. On first and 10 at the Raiders' 26, he took a pitch, swept left, reversed his direction when he spotted safety Ken Coffey closing in, circled back to the middle, and cut upfield.

Suddenly, he was in the open and on his way to a 74-yard touchdown run, which helped earn him most valuable player honours.

Theme art by James Endicott

SCORING SUMMARY:

Washington	0	3	6	0	9
L.A. Raiders	7	14	14	3	38

Raiders – Jensen recovered blocked punt in end zone (Bahr kick)
Raiders – Branch 12 pass from Plunkett (Bahr kick)
Wash – FG Moseley 24
Raiders – Squirek 5 interception return (Bahr kick)
Wash – Riggins 1 run (kick blocked)
Raiders – Allen 5 run (Bahr kick)
Raiders – Allen 74 run (Bahr kick)
Raiders – FG Bahr 21

Richard Mackson

George Rose

San Francisco's Roger Craig

**January 20, 1985
Palo Alto, California**

In a duel of two of the most celebrated quarterbacks of the 1980s, Joe Montana emerged as the winning signal caller and most valuable player in **San Francisco's** surprisingly easy 38-16 victory over **Miami** at Stanford Stadium.

The passing statistics tell much of the story of the game:

— Forced by a weak ground game to pass on almost every play in the second half, Miami's Dan Marino was 29 of 50 for 318 yards, one touchdown, and was intercepted twice. Not as quick as Montana and under pressure from the 49ers, he was sacked four times.

— Able to mix his team's passing and running attacks and running himself for 59 yards and a touchdown on 5 carries, Montana also threw 35 times with 24 completions for 331 yards and 3 touchdowns.

"All week, all we heard was, 'Miami, Miami, Miami,'" Montana said. "That motivated us. We felt we had more tools than Miami — passing, running, a great defence — and we wanted to prove it."

Miami actually led at the start of the game on a 37-yard field goal by Uwe von Schamann.

It didn't take the 49ers long to grab the lead. On the next series Montana contributed a key 15-yard run to a drive that climaxed when he hit running back Carl Monroe with a 33-yard touchdown pass for a 7-3 lead.

Keena Turner (58) and Michael Carter (95) wrap up Nat Moore

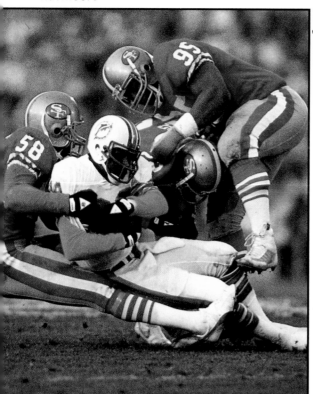

Theme art by Baron Wolfman

Miami looked as dangerous as ever when Marino countered with a 70-yard drive in six plays. The touchdown was scored on his two-yard pass to tight end Dan Johnson, and the Dolphins led 10-7.

More than three quarters of football remained, but for Miami it was all over.

In the second quarter, the 49ers reeled off three touchdowns, while all Miami could counter with was 31 and 30-yard field goals by von Schamann. The Dolphins were shut out in the second half.

The 49ers' second-quarter explosion included an eight-yard touchdown pass from Montana to Roger Craig, a six-yard scoring run by Montana, and a two-yard run for a score by Craig.

SCORING SUMMARY:

Miami	10	6	0	0	16
San Francisco	7	21	10	0	38

Mia – FG von Schamann 37
SF – Monroe 33 pass from Montana (Wersching kick)
Mia – D. Johnson 2 pass from Marino (von Schamann kick)
SF – Craig 8 pass from Montana (Wersching kick)
SF – Montana 6 run (Wersching kick)
SF – Craig 2 run (Wersching kick)
Mia – FG von Schamann 31
Mia – FG von Schamann 30
SF – FG Wersching 27
SF – Craig 16 pass from Montana (Wersching kick)

Tim Alexander

William Perry (72)

January 26, 1986
New Orleans, Louisiana

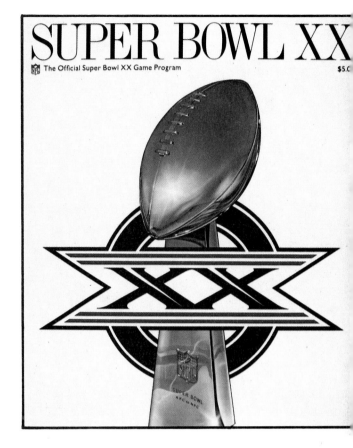

SUPER BOWL XX

The Official Super Bowl XX Game Program

$5.0

In the twentieth Super Bowl, **New England** took a 3-0 first-quarter lead, and then was blitzed by the **Chicago Bears,** who won the most one-sided game in Super Bowl history, 46-10. The Bears gained 408 yards in offence, but mainly they overpowered the Patriots with their aggressive defence.

The Bears' defence forced six turnovers, returned an interception for a touchdown, scored a safety, had seven sacks, and held the Patriots to 123 yards and a Super Bowl-record-low seven yards on the ground.

Bears defensive end Richard Dent, who had 1 1/2 sacks, three other tackles, two forced fumbles, and a pass deflection, was named the most valuable player.

Meanwhile, quarterback Jim McMahon directed a Bears offence that produced four long scoring drives in the Superdome. With wide receiver Willie Gault as his main target (four catches for 129 yards), McMahon connected on 12 of 20 passes for 256 yards.

A Walter Payton fumble, recovered by linebacker Don Blackmon, allowed the Patriots to score first. The turnover gave New England the ball on Chicago's 19-yard line, but three incomplete passes led only to a 36-yard field goal by Tony Franklin and a 3-0 lead.

The Bears, who had a 15-1 regular season record, came right back to tie the score. A 43-yard pass from McMahon to Gault set up a 28-yard field goal by Kevin Butler.

A pair of turnovers late in the first quarter allowed the Bears to take charge of the game. First, Dent sacked New England quarterback Tony Eason, who fumbled the ball away at his own 13. Butler kicked a 24-yard field goal to give the Bears a 6-3 lead.

On New England's first play after the kick-off, running back Craig James fumbled and linebacker Mike Singletary recovered for the Bears. On second down, running back Matt Suhey went 11 yards for the score and a 13-3 Chicago lead.

The rout was on. McMahon scored from the two in the second quarter and Butler added a 24-yard field goal to make it 23-3 at half-time, but the worst was still to come for the American Conference champion Patriots.

The Bears added 21 unanswered points in the third quarter before the Patriots scored their only touchdown late in the game.

SCORING SUMMARY:

Chicago	13	10	21	2	46
New England	3	0	0	7	10

NE – FG Franklin 36
Chi – FG Butler 28
Chi – FG Butler 24
Chi – Suhey 11 run (Butler kick)
Chi – McMahon 2 run (Butler kick
Chi – FG Butler 24
Chi – McMahon 1 run (Butler kick)
Chi – Phillips 28 interception return (Butler kick)
Chi – Perry 1 run (Butler kick)
NE – Fryar 8 pass from Grogan (Franklin kick)
Chi – Safety, Waechter tackled Grogan in end zone

Chicago Defensive End Richard Dent (95)

John E. Biever

SUPER BOWL XXI

AFC vs. NFC for the NFL Championship and the Vince Lombardi Trophy • Sunday, January 25, 1987 • 3:00 PM • Rose Bowl, Pasadena, California

Programme cover art by Chris Hopkins

January 25, 1987
Pasadena, California

The game was 30 minutes too long for Denver's American Conference champions. At half-time, the **Broncos** held a 10-9 advantage and should have had more. Quarterback John Elway had run the proud **New York Giants** ragged, and passed them silly with 13 completions in 20 attempts for 187 yards.

Thirty minutes later the Giants were Super Bowl champions with a 39-20 victory before 101,063 at the Rose Bowl.

Instead of Elway, the most valuable player was New York quarterback Phil Simms. With Denver's defence geared to stop running back Joe Morris, Simms had a record afternoon. He completed all 10 of his second-half passes and an unbelievable 22 of 25 overall for 268 yards and three touchdowns.

Elway also showed his greatness, hitting 22 of 37 for 304 yards and a touchdown, but he didn't have the ground game to match New York's.

The Broncos had fun for a while. Rick Karlis got them in front in the first quarter with a Super Bowl-record 48 yard field goal. Then, after a six-yard pass from Simms to tight end Zeke Mowatt put the Giants ahead, 7-3, Elway scored on a four-yard run to reclaim the lead, 10-7.

No one suspected then that the Broncos wouldn't score again until the fourth quarter. One of the reasons was the surprising loss of effectiveness by the Denver kicker, Rich Karlis, who missed easy 23- and 34-yard field-goal tries late in the first half.

Denver's John Elway (7) comes up against Leonard Marshall (70)

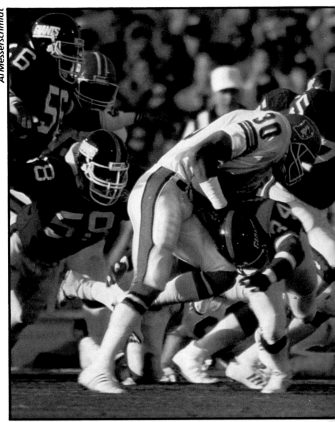

Lawrence Taylor (56), Steve Sewell (30), Carl Banks (58), George Martin (75)

Coach Bill Parcells regrouped his Giants in the dressing room at half-time, and they then outscored the Broncos 30-3, before Denver scored a meaningless touchdown with two minutes left.

Among the 10 consecutive passes Simms completed in the second half were scoring passes of 13 yards to tight end Mark Bavaro and six yards to wide receiver Phil McConkey. By the end of the third quarter New York was ahead 26-10 and it was just a question of how bad the rout would be.

SCORING SUMMARY:

Denver	10	0	0	10	20
New York Giants	7	2	17	13	39

Den — FG Karlis 48
NY — Mowatt 6 pass from Simms (Allegre kick)
Den — Elway 4 run (Karlis kick)
NY — Safety, Elway sacked by Martin
NY — Bavaro 13 pass from Simms (Allegre kick)
NY — FG Allegre 21
NY — Morris 1 run (Allegre kick)
NY — McConkey 6 pass from Simms (Allegre kick)
Den — FG Karlis 28
NY — Anderson 2 run (kick failed)
Den — V. Johnson 47 pass from Elway (Karlis kick)

Doug Williams sets up to pass

**January 31, 1988
San Diego, California**

In many ways, **Denver's** second consecutive appearance in the Super Bowl was a reprise of the first. Quarterback John Elway was hot again at the start, as the Broncos took a 10-0 lead against the **Washington Redskins.**

And, again, the Broncos faded against a record-setting quarterback and what had looked so promising earlier turned out to be a crushing 42-10 loss.

Elway wasn't nearly as brilliant this time, completing 14 of 38 passes for 257 yards and throwing three interceptions. He did fire a 56-yard touchdown pass to wide receiver Ricky Nattiel on the first play of the game.

But this day belonged to Redskins quarterback Doug Williams, who had spent most of the season as a backup to Jay Schroder. In 1986, Williams had been rescued from the defunct United States Football League after a chequered career with the Tampa Bay Buccaneers.

Going into the game, Williams drew attention as the first black quarterback to start a Super Bowl game. He had a simpler title after the game: most valuable player, after a Super Bowl-record 340 passing yards and four touchdown passes.

An incredible second quarter put Williams and the Redskins in the record book.

After hyperflexing his left knee and being forced to leave the game earlier, Williams came back with his team down 10-0 and 14:17 left in the first half. He threw an 80-yard touchdown pass on his first play and proceeded to lead the Redskins to 35 points in the second quarter, throwing four touchdown passes in all. Washington scored five touchdowns in five series and only 5:47 of possession time.

Theme art by Lisa French

It was unbelievable.

During the spree, Williams tossed 80- and 50-yard touchdown passes to wide receiver Ricky Sanders, a 27-yarder to wide receiver Gary Clark, and an eight-yarder to tight end Clint Didier.

Williams wasn't the only improbable hero. During the regular season, running back Timmy Smith had a total of only 126 yards. With a crowd of 72,302 at Jack Murphy Stadium and a world-wide television audience watching, the running back rambled for touchdown runs of 58 and 4 yards and finished with a Super Bowl-record 204 yards rushing.

Doug Williams (17) and Timmy Smith (36)

Dick Raphael

SCORING SUMMARY:

Washington	0	35	0	7	42
Denver	10	0	0	0	10

Den – Nattiel 56 pass from Elway (Karlis kick)
Den – FG Karlis 24
Wash – Sanders 80 pass from Williams (Haji-Sheikh kick)
Wash – Clark 27 pass from Williams (Haji-Sheikh kick)
Wash – Smith 58 run (Haji-Sheikh kick)
Wash – Sanders 50 pass from Williams (Haji-Sheikh kick)
Wash – Didier 8 pass from Williams (Haji-Sheikh kick)
Wash – Smith 4 run (Haji-Sheikh kick)

Theme art by Chris Hopkins

**January 22, 1989
Miami, Florida**

"**A** day I'll never forget," Jerry Rice said about perhaps the most dramatic Super Bowl ever played – a 20-16 victory for the wide receiver's **San Francisco 49ers** over **Cincinnati.**

Rice, who caught 11 passes for 215 yards and a touchdown, and was chosen most valuable player, will have a lot of company in remembering this game.

John Taylor's winning touchdown catch

Bob Rosato

Bob Rosato

San Francisco Wide Receiver Jerry Rice

– For Joe Montana, the inspirational 49ers quarterback, there will be the memory of a 92-yard drive for the winning touchdown with 34 seconds left in the game. Montana completed eight of nine passes on the drive.

– For wide receiver John Taylor it will be his 10-yard catch – his only reception of the game – for the winning touchdown.

For San Francisco coach Bill Walsh it will not only be remembered as his third Super Bowl triumph but his last appearance as a head coach. Several days after the game, Walsh announced his retirement.

Spinelli

Roger Craig

The first 30 minutes of the game were as dull as the final half was dramatic. San Francisco led 3-0 after the first quarter on Mike Cofer's 41-yard field goal. Jim Breech tied it with a 34-yard field goal in the second quarter.

A 43-yard field goal by Breech gave the Bengals a 6-3 lead in the third quarter, but Cofer matched it with a 32-yarder to tie it up again, with 50 seconds left in the third quarter.

And then the game plot turned into a stirring drama. Cincinnati's Stanford Jennings returned the next kick-off 93 yards for a touchdown to give the Bengals a 13-6 lead.

The game was just warming up. On the 49ers' next possession, Montana hit running back Roger Craig with a 40-yard pass and then Rice with a 14-yard touchdown throw. San Francisco 13, Cincinnati 13.

Later in the fourth quarter, after driving from their own 32 to the 49ers' 22, the Bengals sent out Breech to kick a 40-yard field goal for a 16-13 lead.

There was 3:10 left in the game when Montana took over for the most pressure-packed drive of his career on his own 8-yard line. And there were only 34 seconds remaining in the game when Taylor reached up to grab his only pass reception of the game.

SCORING SUMMARY:

Cincinnati	0	3	10	3	16
San Francisco	3	0	3	14	20

SF – FG Cofer 41
Cin – FG Breech 34
Cin – FG Breech 43
SF – FG Cofer 32
Cin – Jennings 93 kickoff return (Breech kick)
SF – Rice 14 pass from Montana (Cofer kick)
Cin – FG Breech 40
SF – Taylor 10 pass from Montana (Cofer kick)

Quarterback Joe Montana

Herb Weitman

The Rose Bowl – Super Bowl XI

New Orleans Superdome – Super Bowl XX

**Rice Stadium –
Super Bowl VIII**

Herb Weitman

Not for the Super Bowl one traditional location!

The selection process for a Super Bowl site is not unlike a beauty contest for cities. The entrants preen for the screening judges, in this case the Super Bowl Site Selection Committee, and later the final judges, the owners of teams in the National Football League.

In the preliminary judging, as many as 20 entrants are allowed only 15 minutes to show off their best attributes.

And just like in the Miss Universe contest only a few make it to the finals where the winner is guaranteed huge amounts of publicity and barrels full of tourist dollars.

The Super Bowl is constantly in motion and only one thing is certain: wherever the game is played, it will be a sellout at $100 for every seat in the stadium.

The main criteria in the judging process are that

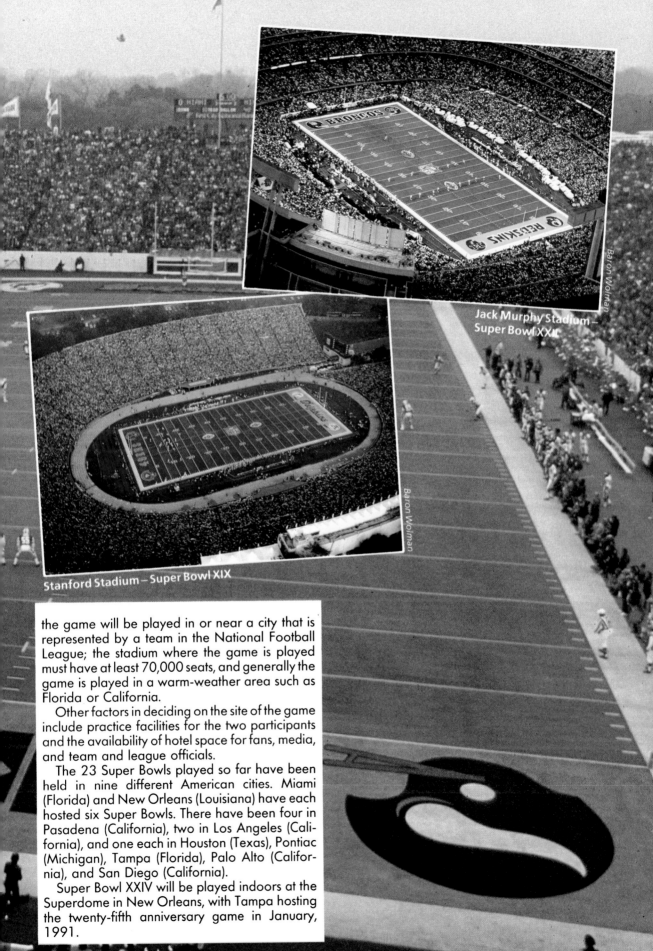

Baron Wolman

Jack Murphy Stadium – Super Bowl XXII

Baron Wolman

Stanford Stadium – Super Bowl XIX

the game will be played in or near a city that is represented by a team in the National Football League; the stadium where the game is played must have at least 70,000 seats, and generally the game is played in a warm-weather area such as Florida or California.

Other factors in deciding on the site of the game include practice facilities for the two participants and the availability of hotel space for fans, media, and team and league officials.

The 23 Super Bowls played so far have been held in nine different American cities. Miami (Florida) and New Orleans (Louisiana) have each hosted six Super Bowls. There have been four in Pasadena (California), two in Los Angeles (California), and one each in Houston (Texas), Pontiac (Michigan), Tampa (Florida), Palo Alto (California), and San Diego (California).

Super Bowl XXIV will be played indoors at the Superdome in New Orleans, with Tampa hosting the twenty-fifth anniversary game in January, 1991.

National Football Conference teams have won the last five Super Bowls, yet American Football Conference teams still hold a slight lead of 12 wins to 11 overall.

There have been only 12 different winners of Super Bowl games. Pittsburgh holds the record with four wins, San Francisco has three, while the Raiders won it twice when based in Oakland and once more after their move to Los Angeles. Green Bay, Dallas, Miami and Washington are two-time winners.

Of the 28 NFL teams, 10 have yet to make it to a Super Bowl, if the Colts' appearances when based in Baltimore are taken into account. The no-show teams are: Atlanta Falcons, Buffalo Bills, Cleveland Browns, Detroit Lions, Houston Oilers, New Orleans Saints, San Diego Chargers, Seattle Seahawks, Tampa Bay Buccaneers and the Cardinals, previously of St. Louis but now from Phoenix.

The Super Bowl so-near-yet-so-far team is Minnesota. The Vikings have represented the National Football Conference four times in the 'World Championship' game – and have lost on each occasion.

Michael Minardi

San Francisco 49ers – pass protection

Manny Rubio

New Orleans Saints
passing from the pocket

1989's game between San Francisco and Cincinnati was the third repeat pairing of Super Bowl contenders. Super Bowls VII and XVII were played between Washington and Miami, each team winning once. Two of Pittsburgh's four victories came against Dallas in Super Bowls X and XIII.

San Francisco's win in Super Bowl XXIII broke an unusual sequence. The 49ers scored first, but in the previous four Super Bowls, the team which scored first had lost!

The half-time score in game XXIII was 3-3 – the first ever tie after two quarters of play. It was the second lowest half-time score in terms of points scored however. Only Super Bowl IX had seen fewer points on the board at the half-way stage – and that was the unusual scoreline of 2-0 to Pittsburgh. Those points came when Fran Tarkenton, the Minnesota quarterback was sacked in his own end zone for a 'safety'.

Of the 23 'World Championship' games, Most Valuable Player awards have gone to the winning quarterback 12 times. Only Super Bowl XII produced two MVPs – Harvey Martin and Randy White, both Defensive linemen for the Dallas Cowboys.

Lamar Hunt, owner of the Kansas City Chiefs, is credited with coining the words 'Super Bowl' to describe America's premier sporting occasion. The title was only adopted in 1969 – the two games before then were referred to by the title 'AFL-NFL World Championship Game'.

Until the Chicago Bears won Super Bowl XX, their division, the NFC Central, had not produced Super Bowl Champions since Green Bay in games I and II. The AFC Eastern Division is now challenging that drought however – it is 15 years since it produced a Super Bowl winning team.

Strongest division – in terms of the number of contenders it has sent to different Super Bowls – is the NFC Eastern Division, which has been represented 11 times.

Venues for each Super Bowl, which are usually different from year to year, are decided upon three years in advance. It is possible for a team to be playing a Super Bowl on its home ground, but this has never happened in the history of the competition.

New Orleans and Miami are the two cities which have staged most Super Bowls. Each city has played host to the big game six times, receiving enormous boosts to local finances on each occasion. For example, New Orleans claims that over $100 million was injected into its economy from Super Bowl XX.

Super Bowl XXIV, to be played on 28th January, 1990, goes back to New Orleans and the Louisiana Superdome. Super Bowl XXV, the silver anniversary 'World Championship', is scheduled to be played on 27th January, 1991, at Tampa Stadium, in Tampa Bay, Florida.

Vernon Biever

Kansas City Chiefs – field goal attempt